On Assignment

On Assignment

Photographs by Jay Maisel

Smithsonian Institution Press, Washington and London
Published in association with Constance Sullivan Editions

This series was developed and produced for Smithsonian Institution Press
by Constance Sullivan Editions

Editors:
Constance Sullivan
Susan Weiley
Designed by Katy Homans

The editors would like to thank Emily Vickers, Studio Manager for Jay Maisel, for her assistance
in the preparation of this book.

First edition

Printed in Italy by TRILOGY S.a.s.

cover: Assignment for United Technologies. Bananas in water, Costa Rica, 1989

Do you make a distinction between personal and commercial work? Or is good work simply good work?

The degree to which you're able to relate the commercial assignment to your personal methods of working, and *don't* have to compromise what you're about visually, is the degree to which you'll be able to do good work. What makes a great job is simply something you would shoot whether or not you were paid to do it. How you structure an assignment so it does what the client wants, satisfies you, and solves his problem at the same time becomes almost conceptual and political, instead of photographic. I try as much as possible to talk with clients who travel with me, and say, "Look, what you've got me doing at this point is something that I wouldn't shoot unless you were paying me. I'll be happy to shoot it, and do the best job I can, but let's try to make it something that's so exciting that I would shoot it anyway."

Do you get assignments where the client says I want you to photograph a certain way?

Yes, many of those. An ideal assignment is when you're given an enormous amount of freedom, you have an understanding client who uses your work well, and you're given a great amount of money. But two out of three isn't bad. If you have those first two you really wouldn't have to worry about the money so much, because it would be such an incredibly privileged life to lead. But unfortunately the third is necessary in order to support those times when you work on the other two without a job. Then there are those assignments that are frightening in their freedom.

Too much is left to you. There's a saying that a husband is a lover with his nerves gone, with his sensitivity gone. Well sometimes a commercial photographer is a photographer with his sensitivity numbed. For years you are told, "The product has to show, the theme has to be evident, you've got to have a point of view, we want to make ourselves evident." And then somebody comes along and says, "Now forget all that, do whatever you want." And you say, "But in what context?" "No no. What*ever* you want." It takes a long time to get rid of that callus that says there must be a trick somewhere. When somebody sincerely tells you to do something without a context, it's hard to believe. I had a talk with Ernst Haas two or three weeks before he died. We did a campaign separately and together. He did it one year, I did it the next. I asked him, "Were you able to do anything you wanted to?" Because that's the way I had done it. He said, "No, I have always found that if you do it the way *you* want, they very often don't think it's the way *they* want. So I asked them, 'What do you want?' and they told me, and I did what they wanted, and they were *enormously* happy."

How did it happen that *you* were given such freedom?

On that particular assignment I had an art director, John Short, who was influenced by certain things that happened. This was for a campaign called "Born in America." They were doing a film commercial, and I was hired to do the stills for a magazine ad. We had, as they do in advertising, a scenario. They said they wanted this kind of shot, that kind of shot. I went to Athens, Georgia, and I shot; I went to Detroit, I went to Ketchum, Idaho. I met up with the art director in San Diego. He said, "I've been traveling with the film crew, and you know, they stop people in the street, and they don't do it all planned, the way I asked you to do it. I'd really like you to do it that way." So for a good portion of the rest of the shoot, that's just what I did. I just did a lot of free spots.

Some of the things I did on my own they used, some they didn't; but just about everything they had *asked* me to do they used. Because one of the conceptual problems you have with advertising people is the pre-visualized concept. But this art director was willing to let this go by the boards. The best art directors I know realize that when you go out with a concept, and you're wedded to that concept, the best thing that can happen is you're going to get that concept. But if you go out freer, you might get something even better. That's really almost marketing or selling the thing, because it has to do with how the agency instructs the account executive or the client. They might say, "Look, we got better, look at it." But if he's married to the idea, he might answer, "I don't want better. I want what I was promised."

When you work with an advertising agency, does the art director have a very definite preconception, of what the subject should be and how it should look?

No. That doesn't happen often. I've paid enough dues so nobody tells me exactly the way something should look. But there are times when they have a layout, and they want that layout fairly rendered; but I don't often do stuff where layouts are rendered. Basically somebody comes to me because they feel I can express an idea they have, and can do something more.

Once you're on location, they allow you flexibility?

Most people allow you flexibility in terms of the visual thing, but don't often give you freedom in terms of the whole concept. Now they have to go back and sell it, and some guy might say, "Wait a minute. I wanted red and you're giving me blue." But they're willing to try it. I'll give you an example. One client of mine, United Technologies, had a wind-turbine division, and there was nothing to take pictures of because it hadn't been built yet. But they were going to build it, or they had the rights for it. So they said, "Why don't we show what wind could do to nature?" So I said "Okay, I'll go to Big Sur and other places where trees have been bent double by nature." So I did a whole series of trees bent double by wind, or I went someplace where a whole line of trees was angled by wind. But on my way back I saw people hang-gliding, and I told them I thought they should use the hang-glider, because what they're really concerned with is what *man* does with wind, not what nature does with wind. And they said, "Yes, it makes more sense."

Why would an art director hire a photographer with your reputation and stature and then tell you what to do?

It doesn't happen that often, but it's a question I have talked about at great length. I have often told art directors, "If you're going to hire me and pay me a lot of money, you're not getting your money's worth if you don't at least let me do what I want to do *before* you tell me what you want me to do. If you feel that way, what you should do is get somebody very young, somebody just starting, and tell him exactly what to do so he'll render it for you the way you want it. Or become a photographer yourself." But I think that what you're involved with a great many times is that everything is motivated by fear. These guys are making an enormous sum of money from an agency that is making an enormous sum of money, and there's a lot riding on it. And they're terrified.

Did you have to go through that stage when you were starting? Did you have to pay your dues?

I think the thing that saved me was the fact that I was technically incompetent to do what they wanted. I had to be creative. I had no choice. I was never really able to bullshit. I remember an art director at McCann-Erickson my first couple of years in the business. He said, "We're going to send you out to do an ad for Esso. I want you to come back with a great photograph. Can you come back with a great photograph?" Now I'm twenty-four years old and I'm thinking, Is this guy crazy? I said, "I don't know. I'll *try*. . . . I mean, I'll *try* to come back with a great photograph." But he said, "Can you *guarantee* me you'll come back with a great photograph?" You know, I'm looking around at the other people in the room, nobody's giving me any signs like, tell him you're going to get a good photograph. "Yeah!" I finally said. "I'll come back with a great photograph. Okay?"

This was a hell of an assignment. It was a very simple assignment of a car stopped at a light in the evening. Only this guy put some very rigid limitations on it. It had to be an orange car. How many orange cars do you see? In the 1950s? It took me a week to find two orange cars. I hired them *both* to come down. Then he wanted autumn leaves in the picture. It was summer. At that time you could not buy autumn leaves. I mean today you can buy them. But at that time you couldn't. It just so happened that I've been a collector from a very early age, and I had an entire collection of autumn leaves. So I used my autumn leaves.

Oh, there was one little thing about the shot: the art director had *no* understanding of visual things, or the laws of optics. He wanted a traffic light reflected in the autumn leaves—and he wanted it reflected in a perfect circle. But it doesn't work that way. If you have a still pool of water, you get a perfect reflection; but as you know, when you look at the moon on the ocean, it's reflected as a line. I stood there twenty minutes trying to explain that to him. He didn't understand. Anyway, so I had a flusher wagon. I had the police department. I had the fire department. I had the sanitation department. I had the reflection. And I had traffic backed up on Second Avenue for about forty blocks. And I had a little Hasselblad camera at the time. I didn't have a big camera. So I did the shot, they bounced it. They hired another guy, he did the shot, they bounced it. I was still friendly with the people up there so I suggested, "Why don't you do it in a model-maker's studio, so you can control everything the way you want it?" So they did it in the model-maker's studio, and they bounced it. It was in the days when money didn't matter, and they would do things over and over. But it never ran.

Do art directors usually know about photography?

Some know about photography. Others figure the more they know about photography the more they'll be willing to accept excuses, so they don't want to know anything about it. In other words, an expert is someone who knows it can't be done. They don't want to become experts. They'd rather remain the naive person who can then say, "I want it the way I want it because I want it, and I don't want to hear any excuses."

Are there any assignments that you especially like?

I like the free assignments better than the unfree assignments. But I'm looking at this from the point of view of someone who's been in the business a long time. When I started, I liked any assignment. I used to go up to a place and saturate it. In other words, they were going to hire me. I sat in BBD&O's offices for a week and a half, and I saw every art director there. And I had *lots* of work to show. It didn't work. I didn't get anything. But I'd given it my best shot. I remember haunting J. Walter Thompson; I sat there for four days bugging everybody. A month later I finally got something. I looked at the assignment and I looked at my work, and I wondered, "Do they know who this is?" Because everything I had was outdoors, using available light, and they wanted me to shoot a woman lifting up a curtain in a studio. At that time I had *no idea* how to use light. I was about twenty-four, twenty-five. So I just made them wait a week and a half until the light was right. I had to use available light. I couldn't do that today.

How did you start? Did you think, I want to be an advertising photographer?

No. I didn't do advertising for the first few years I was in the business. I never wanted to be any particular kind of photographer, I just wanted to take pictures. That was what was important. The first pictures I took were medical pictures for pharmaceutical houses. And album covers. Advertising came at a much later date. I never was interested in doing the kind of advertising that I thought was tacky. I was always looking for the few great assignments that they had.

You studied painting at Yale. How did you get from painting to photography?

The transition from painting to photography was one of those things where you have to take into account my personality, which prefers instant gratification. It's very easy to get that from a photograph, and very difficult to get it from a painting that you have to work on for months at a time. And painting didn't come easily to me.

Were you looking at photography at that time? Were you looking at other peoples' work?

I had no contact with other photographers, but I'd seen their work. I'd seen Henri Cartier-Bresson's work and loved it, because the pictures didn't always answer questions, they asked questions. I loved Arnold Newman's work. I looked at his photograph of Stravinsky with the piano, and that was it. It was really a great picture.

Because it did something with photography that you didn't know could be done?

It just moved me. I wasn't able to intellectualize about it. It made me say, "Okay, photography can do something that's great. I want to take pictures." I learned pretty much on my own. I photographed extensively with very little background in the beginning. I had a book by Andreas Feininger called *Introduction to Photography*, and I zealously devoured it. That was my instruction. Whatever formal instruction was available seemed pathetic. The only formal instruction I had was a class I took with Herbert Matter at Yale. He was a great photographer, but he couldn't teach at all. But two or three years before I took his course I lived next to him. One night I woke up and heard this weird music. I thought I was dreaming because I'd never heard anything like this before. The next day I heard the music during the afternoon. A chill went up my arm, so I ran next door. Matter always had a cigarette hanging from his mouth; it killed him at about the age of ninety. So he opened the door. "Yeeesss?" I told him I thought I was dreaming. "Oh no. This is a movie I did on Alexander Calder. The music is by a man named John Cage." So I said, "Can I come in?" What I got out of him was looking at what he did. He was a man of enormous intensity, enormous privacy, and enormous competence. I learned a lot from him. But his course was less than useful.

After I became a photographer I took a course with Alexey Brodovitch. That was wonderful. Brodovitch was never a photographer, but he'd done some great photographs. He was inspirational. He was, after all, *Brodovitch*. When you met him you knew you were in the presence of someone there was a whole legend about, so you listened to him. But Brodovitch made you work.

One of the things he did was explain to you that you have an obligation to yourself: you must not go out and shoot the job just for the client, you must shoot it for yourself also. I switched it around to: if you just photograph to satisfy your client you're short-changing him. If you don't also satisfy your-self, you're giving him less than you'd be happy with. Brodovitch stimulated you. He wouldn't take any crap. He'd look at something and he'd say, "This is garbage, and you have to do this, that, and the other thing to make it work." He wouldn't look for pat, easy solutions. He did not accept excuses of any kind. He didn't want to know if somebody died in the family or if you'd lost an arm that day. It didn't matter.

What is important to you about photography: what do you think makes a good photograph? What do you feel distinguishes you from somebody whose work you despise, or somebody who is out there just making a lot of money?

There's no visual criteria that I could use to answer you. I think the kind of people who are motivated solely by a desire to make a living at it, really don't like it, and if they could would be doing something else. I know people like that, and I'm friendly with them on a business level. But what makes a photo-graph good is the kind of passion that goes into it. If it's not passion, then it's intellect. If it's not intellect, it's wit. If it's not passion or intellect or wit then it's some kind of color sense. There's always some aspect of a good photo-graph that raises it above the average, and it's not possible to say it's only one single thing. It may be that a particular man like Doisneau or Brassaï or Frank or Cartier-Bresson has an ability to see those moments in which we reveal ourselves as human beings. And that kind of insight is what makes it a great photograph. And so it may be with Irving Penn or Ernst Haas, that there is a visual wit and sophistication in graphic terms. In other cases it's just the hu-manity that people have. When I saw Penn's *Moments Observed*, I cried. And there are no words in it. It's just great portraits.

I think what makes a great photograph is that it evokes something, it hits that tuning fork, that thing that's sympathetic. It's the same thing that makes a great performance. What makes a great photograph for me is some-thing that evokes a personal response. It could be intellectual or emotional.

When your photographs are greatly enlarged and exhibited on a wall, they resemble paintings. They have an "all-over" quality that is related to the whole school of modernism in art—particularly the New York School of painting—where every inch of the surface is filled, and is alive. Obviously it's conscious.

One of the places where a lot of photographers fail is in their inability to be responsible for every part of the picture. It's like, I'm in charge of the foreground, God can take care of the background. That's what screws up a lot of pictures. Background and foreground are not two different things.

Is it something you pay attention to in your commercial work as well as in your personal work?

I try. It's more difficult there. Greg Heisler talks about this in a much funnier way than I can. He says, "We'll sit down in the first meeting on a project. I don't know the designer, the designer doesn't know me. None of us has any idea where we're going to go to shoot, the project is not going to take place for two months, we don't know what country it's going to be in, or even what the subject matter is—but I've got to have a long vertical. That might be very difficult, because we have to shoot the Queen Mary. And the next day it has to be a horizontal, and that could be difficult because we have to shoot the Eiffel Tower." So it's hard to look as good commercially as you can when you have complete control over your work. You may be in a situation where you have absolutely no control over how they use your picture. Somebody might think, "You mean you allow them to do that?" Well man, once you take the money you've got an obligation to let them do what they want; you may or may not have input, and you may realize they're screwing up, but that's the way it is. For example, the art director I referred to from the shoot in Ketchum and Athens had put together a very nice layout, almost a pastiche in Rauschenberg terms, of the way pictures were going to be used. It was good. When the final thing came together they didn't let him do it the way he wanted; they wanted hard edges where he wanted soft, they wanted this picture where they wanted that picture, and there's not much he could do about it. That's why they call it "selling out."

How closely do you edit your pictures before you submit them to a client?

Very closely. The strange thing is that I would edit much tighter except I feel I can edit only up to a certain point and then it's really up to the art director, not to me. I'm going to give him a matrix, and within it everything he could possibly want is there. But I don't know which one he should use.

You wouldn't ever give an art director the possibility of using a picture that you yourself were not happy with?

No. Matter of fact, that's one of the key talks I give. I would say the most frequently used phrase among photographers in the commercial business is, "They used the wrong picture." And what I say is, "How did they get it?" As a matter of fact, one of the ways I edit is, I look at the picture and I think, "Would I want my name under that? Am I going to show it to them so I look like I shot a little more? Or is it because I really want them to use it? Would I show this to the person I admire the most, or would I be self-conscious about showing it?" But I cannot edit it down to the best shot.

What if you take a photograph that you think is perfectly composed, and they crop it radically?

It doesn't usually happen with me. It may happen with other people. There have been occasions, with a very good art director, when something has happened and the reasons have been incredible. I had a picture of a sunset with a barn and a cow and an airplane in the middle of everything on top. They printed it without the airplane. I asked why. "Aw, it was too much." I used to do the bathing suit issues for *Sports Illustrated*. I did the first one and three others. The last one I did I was so furious about the layout—up until then they had good layouts and the same art director—but this time they got cute. They cut a circle out of Cheryl Tiegs's stomach and put another photograph inside of that, used crazy shapes, and so on. Afterward I went to them and said, "I love working with you guys, but I'll never work for you again unless I have layout approval." So I never worked for them again. You can't expect good treatment from someone who's giving you bad treatment unless you specify it, and unless you're willing to walk away.

When you give workshops or work with young people, what do they want to know? What kind of information do they expect? Do they want to know how to become a rich, successful photographer? How you did it?

Nobody has ever asked how I did it. They ask things like "What film do you use?" "What kind of camera do you use?" The intelligent ones ask how I approach certain problems that come up now. But if they did ask about that, I would try to explain to them that it's a very different business now. I was one of maybe a couple of hundred photographers of any substance in New York when I started. Now there are thousands.

Has the technology made it too easy to just point and shoot?

More than that, it has been so glamorized. It seems like a *wonderful* way to make a living. I think people have a degree of sophistication about visual things, and like me, are not really competent enough to be painters. But photography offers an easy marriage of technology and art. They'll be able to be artists, but they won't have to know how to draw a hand. And they'll travel to exotic lands. It's better than working in a factory or working on a computer.

What about the notion that anybody can make pictures, that it's just a technical thing, that the camera makes the pictures?

I think it's bullshit. The camera is one link. To say that it's the camera only is to negate other links in the chain. You don't have to physically know how to draw the hand or eye or face or mountain, so there's a lot less physical difficulty in it. But it's only a link. The degree of difficulty in execution is not the criterion of art, otherwise we would all worship paintings done on the head of a pin.

But some very intelligent people who are otherwise sensitive and thoughtful, say, "Photography is so simple it can't be art, you just hold up the camera, you take the picture. What's the big deal?"

They know an entire painting career takes a lot of planning, a lot of craft, and there's a lot of residual and instinctive resentment because photography looks easy. There's a feeling that you have to earn these things. I used to work for Bucky Fuller. He would never prepare a speech, because he felt that whatever you got up to say, your whole life was a preparation for that speech. I had a painter-teacher who felt the same way. He said, "You don't prepare a painting, you prepare your life. The painting comes out of your life." That's what happens with photographs too. If I walked down a street with five other photographers with cameras, we're all going to see different things, and take five different pictures. We have five different attitudes—and it's the attitude that it has taken time to develop.

You said when you first started you didn't know anything about lighting, and you just waited for days for the available light to be right. Could photographers starting out today get away with that?

Today it's not an issue of whether they could get away with it or not. The issue is how much more sophisticated they are today. I would say ten times more. They will know more visually than I know. Sometimes I have assistants who know more than I do. I ask them questions. They say, "You don't *know* that?" No, but I know other things that are valuable. I don't think anybody today can get away with being unsophisticated in a market that has so many sophisticated people in it. But that isn't to say that because they have technical ability they're going to be highly successful. It's just that they can't get a foot in the door without it.

One often hears of successful photographers who don't know that much technically.

Well you know, actually there isn't all that much to know. There's a mystique that people build up about it. If you have to light something the size of a football field, then you've got to know a little bit about lighting, and you might want a lighting guy to help you so you don't blow out the city of Pittsburgh. But after all, how complicated is it to know where to put lights? It's something that you look at, do it by trial and error. The technically difficult things people make an issue about are easy to learn. The things that are *important* are the things they don't talk about.

Or that can't be taught.

Yes. Like the ability to see a picture as a whole, and to understand the reason behind the picture. To relate not to your own visual predilection, but to what the subject calls for. For example, Greg Heisler is a young guy who has changed a lot of things because he lights everything. I use his assistant very often, and I'll turn to him and ask how Greg would do the shot. "Exactly like you do, but with lights and filters." Our attitudes are the same, but the way of getting the shot is very different. Greg has spawned a generation of imitators who work not as well as he but who *light* things. A kid coming up today who doesn't know how to light has real problems. And yet what Greg does is so different from what his imitators do, because he responds to each individual object. They assume there is just one way to do it.

How did you teach yourself studio lighting? Or how did you learn it?

My lighting is very unsophisticated. It relates to available light. In other words, I will notice what excites me with available light, and if I want a certain type of effect I'll duplicate that. I try not to do lighting that doesn't envision a reality, because I think that makes a kind of intellectual demand on people that has nothing to do with the kind of pictures I take. If, however, I were doing a picture of a futuristic fantasy, maybe I would try to light it another way, normally. I want my lighting to have some kind of a nostalgic frame of reference—I want people to have *experienced* that light, or think it's so exciting that they *wish* they had.

Joseph Hirsch, the painter I studied with, got me involved with that; he said you should know by looking at a painting what time of day it is, and what time of year it is. You should know how much it cost the man in the painting to buy that suit, and how long it's been worn. He was by no means a magic realist, but he was very involved with that minutiae of information that we are aware of and he wanted to transmit it.

Even though your photographs are the result of a spontaneous response to the subject, they are so carefully composed they appear to be preconceived.

One of the things Garry Winogrand and I used to argue about is he'd say, "Jay feels that his pictures can't have any chaos in them. And the world is full of chaos, so Jay is not really relating to the world." My answer was, yes, the world is full of chaos but I have no obligation to reflect that chaos. Sometimes I want to but I'm not obliged to, any more than I'm obliged to show the sorry plight of mankind in my pictures. There's a lot to be said for what's beautiful. When I'm teaching I tell students there are several levels of sophistication in taking a photograph. The least sophisticated is when you're looking through the magazine, you see your picture, and you realize, "My God, there's something wrong with that picture." The next level is while you're showing it to your client. The next level is when you see it while you are editing the picture. The level above that is when you put the camera up to your eye you see it. I try to teach them to catch it at that early stage. And it can't be an intellectual decision. You have to get to the point that it irritates you *so much* that something is wrong that you can't take the picture.

There's an innate visual respect for a thing that we're talking about. I'm trying to get the kids in my classes to realize that they're responsible for everything in the picture, and that if the picture doesn't work in some way, nobody looking at it may understand *why* it doesn't work, but there's going to be something about it that is off. The total effect is gone. It's like static on the radio: you can still hear the program but there is something wrong and it takes away your enjoyment.

But you have to know when to let go of it too. There are certain situations where it doesn't count anymore. If something incredible is happening in terms of narrative and you're worried about cropping, you're missing the whole point.

How much does your personality contribute to your work? You are very outgoing, demonstrative, warm. And you are big. You have a physical and personal dynamism. How much do these affect the way you photograph?

I try not to intrude on people. I have a philosophy about photographing. It's hard to impart this in ten seconds, but sometimes you have to. It goes, "Look buddy, if I didn't think you're beautiful, I wouldn't photograph you."

Do you use a telephoto lens for your street portraits?

Sometimes. But I think some of my best portraits happen when I'm three feet away. I feel that photographing is an act of love—I really do. You don't waste time and money and film on something you don't like unless you're either a disturbed personality or a crusading photographer, and I'm neither. I'm also involved in the pleasure of the graphics, and with what happens with light and color.

You have a tremendous range of subject matter and you treat it all convincingly. Do you think that's unusual?

I think any good photographer can do anything he wants to do, with the limitation that he might not be able to do a highly technical specialty such as Beauty, because he might be unaware that there are no beauties—beauty photographs are lit and made up and retouched. You might start as a beginning photographer and think, "How come I can never find a woman with skin like that?" Or with an underwater shot, you might think you need to be a David Doubile to do that. If I had to assign ten photographers to shoot ten different things, I would not hesitate to pick ten generalists; good generalists can do anything. One of the jokes about this business is that if you want to photograph left-handed pitchers in a baseball situation there's no point in trying for the job if you have a portfolio of right-handed pitchers. But I don't believe it. For instance, I wouldn't hesitate to send Greg Heisler out to shoot anything, or Stephen Wilkes or Co Rentmeester. If you're good you're good—as long as you're interested in doing it.

Most commercial photographers use assistants. What does an assistant do?

Assistants come with me on jobs. They take care of equipment at all times, carry things, save receipts, and arrange whatever has to be arranged, lay their bodies down in front of an automobile when one comes along. They are primarily schleppers, camera-loaders and -changers, coordinators if you don't have a coordinator. Basically assistants do everything I do but shoot.

**How do you find assistants. Interview a lot of
people and then just select one?**

There are a few guys who I've used on a free-lance basis. Sometimes you
seek them out and want to hire them because they're good. I interviewed a
fellow the other day, and when we were all finished I said, "Let's throw this
bum out of here, because he's too good to be an assistant." He was too
good, he wouldn't have lasted long because he would have been bored and
moved on. And more than that I wouldn't have done him any good either. He
didn't need me—he had a real good eye, and it would have been a shame if I
had influenced that, because his eye had its own direction. So I asked him if
he had enough money to shoot on his own, and he said yes, so I said,
"Shoot on your own."

Who else is essential to your studio?

My studio manager, Emily Vickers, who is the liaison with clients. She never
goes out with me as an assistant. She might come out on a job, but she
wouldn't be an assistant, ever. I don't know if she even knows how. She's the
business manager and the director of the files.

Do you usually charge a day rate?

Either a day rate or a usage rate, whichever is higher. This comes from magazine photography, which is space or day rate, whichever is more. In other
words, I went out for *Life* and did this article on X and they were going to pay
me a day rate, for two days. But they ran it for eight pages, so they're not
going to pay me by the day, they're going to pay me the page rate. However,
if I'd gone out for them and spent eight days, and they ran only one page,
then they'd pay me by the day. Now in the advertising world there are all kinds
of permutations of that.

**What is the difference between advertising
photography and editorial photography?**

Advertising photography is when you're doing photographs that the agency is
going to buy and put in a print ad. Editorial photography is where you get

very little money. Magazines, books. Theoretically, editorial gives you more freedom. But I never looked for a lot of editorial work because I never found a magazine that told somebody, "Go down South, see what's happening." What they really said was, "We have this attitude toward what's going on down South right now. Go down and reinforce it." And if you come back with something that said the exact opposite of what their polemical attitude was, they're not going to publish it. So I never felt you had any more freedom. In fact, I felt you were a lackey for very little money instead of a whore for a lot of money. I thought I was better off being a whore for a lot of money.

Did you ever work in black and white?

I started in black and white and didn't stop working in it seriously until after 1964. The first ten years I shot primarily in black and white. Up to that time I had shot about 5,000 rolls of black and white; after that I stuck with color.

Do you make the prints from your slides yourself?

No, I have somebody else do it. I have enough trouble just controlling the printing process while somebody else does it. I have about as much control as I would have if I had somebody working for me, and a lot more control than if I were doing it myself, because I wouldn't have the patience for it. You've got to know your own limitations. I do *not* like working in the darkroom. I do *not* like being involved with any kind of routine darkroom work. There are a lot of guys who just *love* to get into the darkroom. I don't. I never liked it. I've always felt that everything that is really important about a photograph happens before you shoot it, or at the moment you shoot it. What happens afterward is simply a matter of getting it on paper.

How much more expensive is it for someone who is just opening a studio than when you started? In other words, how much riskier is it to become a commercial photographer today?

I wouldn't want to be starting out today. The average photographer I know who has a studio will be paying anywhere from $2,500 to $4,500 a month rent. That's just the rent. I paid $53.11 for a three-room apartment. When I moved out of that into a 1600-foot studio, I paid $125 a month. We're talking about an *enormous* kind of increase. When I first started shooting in the early 1950s I made from my first good client $300 to $600 a day. Today the rents are so astronomically high—everything is—compared to when I started, and the fees are not that much higher. The top guy in 1954 would make like $2,500; the top guy today would make $5,000. So costs have gone up exponentially, and the fees have maybe doubled.

So how can you make a living?

I think the way the average photographer does it is by cutting down on a lot of things. A lot of photographers don't have studios anymore. Things have changed to the point where they're now beginning to share studios. Some of them rent a studio and bill it to the client. But years ago people would ask, do you have a studio? So I moved into my $125-a-month place so I could answer, "Yes, I have a studio." They never gave me any studio work, but it was important to them that I have a studio. Today guys have to fight for residuals and rights because otherwise they're going to be up the creek. I'm in a little different position, thank god, because I have other sources of income. I can sell stock pictures—I built up a stock library. I can lecture and give workshops. But the guy who's just starting today has the same expenses I have and he doesn't have a big name. The only way he can hope to succeed is if he gets very hot very fast, or if he keeps his expenses way down. Then of course he's got to advertise. There are all these source books, and people seem to feel there's no validity unless you're listed.

But I don't want to grow. I had an argument with a guy who said, if you don't grow you're going to have big trouble. I told him I don't want to get bigger. I want to stay one person, not hiring another photographer to work for me; I tried that once, then I had not just my problems but his problems too. But there's no way you can do without certain things. I used to think it would be nice to cut down on my staff, but somebody's got to run the errands. You can't trust messengers. If your client needs something within the hour, and really needs it, I have to have someone to take it to him. When people say, "What one piece of advice would you give to a young photographer?" I say, "You're not going to believe this, but learn how to make duplicates."

How do you define success?

Success in my terms would be being able to photograph whatever I wanted, whenever I wanted. I'm far away from that.

Without having to think about money?

That's one aspect of it. The other aspect is without having to worry about having the motivation to do it. I happen to be the kind of person who works best under pressure. If something is due on Monday, there's no sense in doing it until Sunday. So possibly if I had no pressure whatsoever . . . If I were really successful I'd be doing a lot more of my own work. I wouldn't stop commercial work. I can see that, as the saying goes, sometimes the worst thing you can have is to get what you want.

How would you assess what you've accomplished?

I went to a shrink at one point, and she said, "I don't know anything about your business, how good are you?" I said, "Okay, I must answer without modesty. I think I'm better than 95% of the people out there. But I'm still not as good as I could be, and I'd like to be that much better." I've asked this question of people I admire, presenting the same conditions—if you were talking to a shrink, not a reporter, how good are you? And it's amazing how many people say, "I would say that I'm better than 90 to 95 percent of the people in my business." Nobody goes over 95, nobody goes under 90. So if you think you're better than 95 percent of the people, you think you're goddamned good. But you can't sit there and say you're great, because you know your shortcomings, you know your failures, you know the things you missed. And you know that you only get a small piece of what you go out for.

client: **United Technologies**
art director: Mark Fennimore
agency: Ogilvy & Mather
location: Costa Rica

This was the toughest physical shoot I have ever done. They wanted the act of cutting down bananas. It's in jungle-like terrain. Every few feet there are irrigation ditches. At any point you step on rotting bananas, and jump over little stumps and logs, because when they cut down a banana plant they leave it to decompose to add nutrients into the land. When you step on these things it's pretty slippery. There are millions of insects, plus spiders as big as your hand about face level as you're walking. But that's the easy part. The tough part is that the banana plants are staked out with diagonal red wire to keep them erect. Sometimes the red disappears and you walk into the wire— they're at 45 degrees so you really have to watch yourself. A guy with a machete measures the bananas to see if they're big enough to cut, and if they're not he goes off in another direction. This guy is lean, doesn't have an ounce of fat on him, and he's used to this. I'm a New York photographer. And I have a 26-year-old assistant. After five minutes we both looked like we were walking out of a shower. This went on for about four hours. Also, we were going from dappled light to sunlight to shade to open shadow to dappled light, and it was a monstrous job to try to keep the exposures on edge.

I wasn't really getting what I wanted. This particular account likes a very graphic look—they're not interested in pictures of people, they want to keep it on an abstract level. I went and watched the whole process. The process is that after they do this, they hook it up to a conveyor belt; the conveyor belt runs to the processing area; in the processing area they take the bananas off the stalk, in fingers of about ten bananas. In order to keep the temperature down, because it's very hot, they soak them in water. Since the client was Carrier Air Conditioning, and they wanted to show how important it was to keep the bananas at a certain temperature, it seemed to me that the cutting down of the plant didn't say anything about temperature control, and the bananas in the temperature-controlled water seemed to make a story. That's the picture they used.

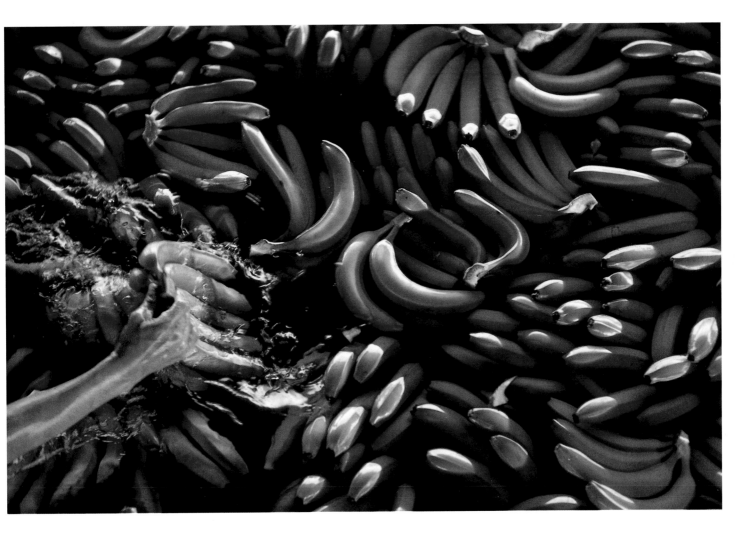

client: **Federal National Mortgage Association**
art director: Larry Bennett
agency: McKinney Silver Rocket, Raleigh, NC
location: Maine

Fannie May was a wonderful assignment, the kind I wish I had more of. It was, "Go and photograph a small town in America and do it with a helicopter." We took a helicopter for four days in the middle of July. It was a shoot that could only be done in the very early morning or late afternoon—in the middle of the day the light gets kind of flat. We scouted where we thought we wanted to shoot—what looked like a great town—then went back toward the end of the day. As the day grew longer, and the light got more dramatic, we really did the best part of the shoot. That was easy. The tough part was finding it again in the morning and waiting for the light to happen. It was a chance to make a statement about the different ways a town looks. Most of the towns we did were in Maine; we felt they were the typical small towns that read immediately as a conglomeration of small to medium-sized homes, which is what Fannie May is all about.

client: **GTE**
art director: Jay Morales
agency: DDB Needham Worldwide Inc.
location: Woodstock, England; New York

We had to photograph a spiderweb, symbolizing a network system; a dandelion with the puffs falling off, representing mobile communication; a bird's egg, which was about the future; the morning glory, showing the power of light; and a child fingerpainting, to demonstrate human touch.

We started researching this, and dandelions were pretty much shot in the United States; bird's eggs wouldn't have been a problem to find; we could have found a spiderweb, but we'd have to go all over the country to do it. Then the client mentioned that they were doing a commercial on the same subject in England, and I decided we should go to England and do it. We were going to have experts gathering up all the things we needed.

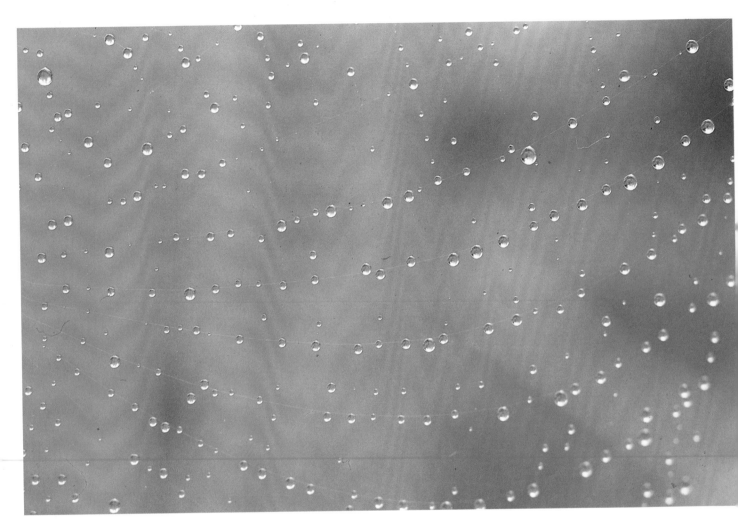

The guy could have said, "Gee, I don't want to fly you and your crew to England." But he said, "Yeah, I think that's a good idea." And we saved him a lot of money, because they already had people doing their scouting. There was somebody there who was the world's leading authority on spiderwebs, and he just gave us spiderwebs every day, and if we wanted a smaller frequency spiderweb he could do that too. For instance, in misting the drops on the web the drops will only get to be a certain size before they fall off. So the concept was to try to make the spiderweb smaller, to show a whole spiderweb with the drops very large. Whereas if it had been a large spiderweb the drops would have been the same size but you wouldn't

client and said, "Look, this looks like hell, and if I work at it I'm going to get a picture that looks like hell. Or I'm not going to get a picture. So I'm leaving here, because I don't think it's do-able. And if it is do-able, it isn't usable, so I don't think it's going to make the point you want to make. Let me think about it on the way back." I realized that they didn't want to show painting, they wanted to show how good their paint was. So the best thing would be to show a detail of a car that reflected something, that showed that the car paint is impervious to water and resists heat, light, cold. I thought I could do that best by showing a reflection in a car with water on it.

client: **N-Ren**
art director: Tom Smith
agency: Griswold Eshleman
location: Sudan, Madagascar

They gave me an enormous amount of freedom on this job, which was "Go to several different countries in Africa and do what you want." It's scary to have all that freedom. So I made sure to give the client a range of things I wanted to do that they could write about. These three pictures relate to the idea of food preparation and consumption.

x

41

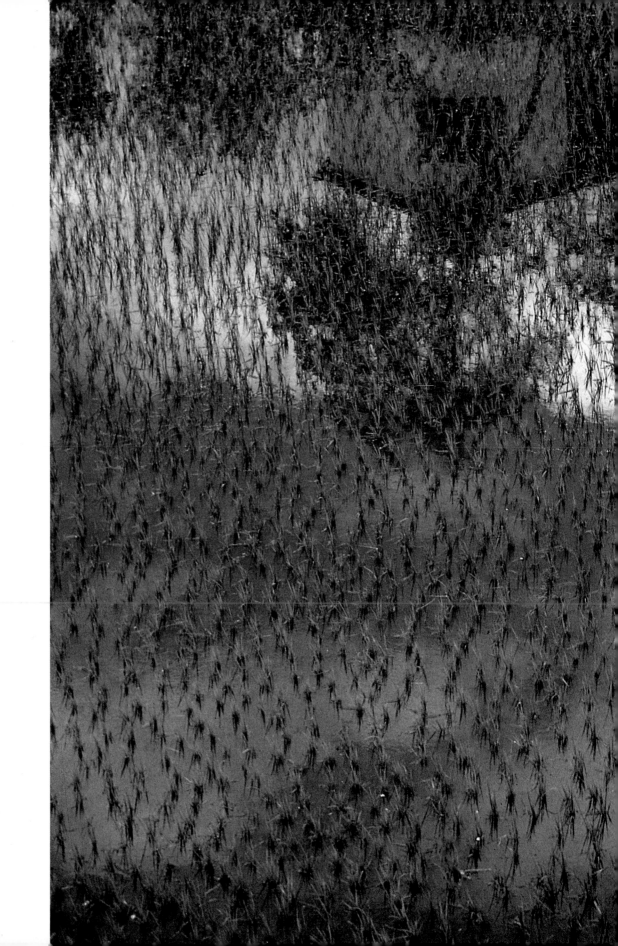

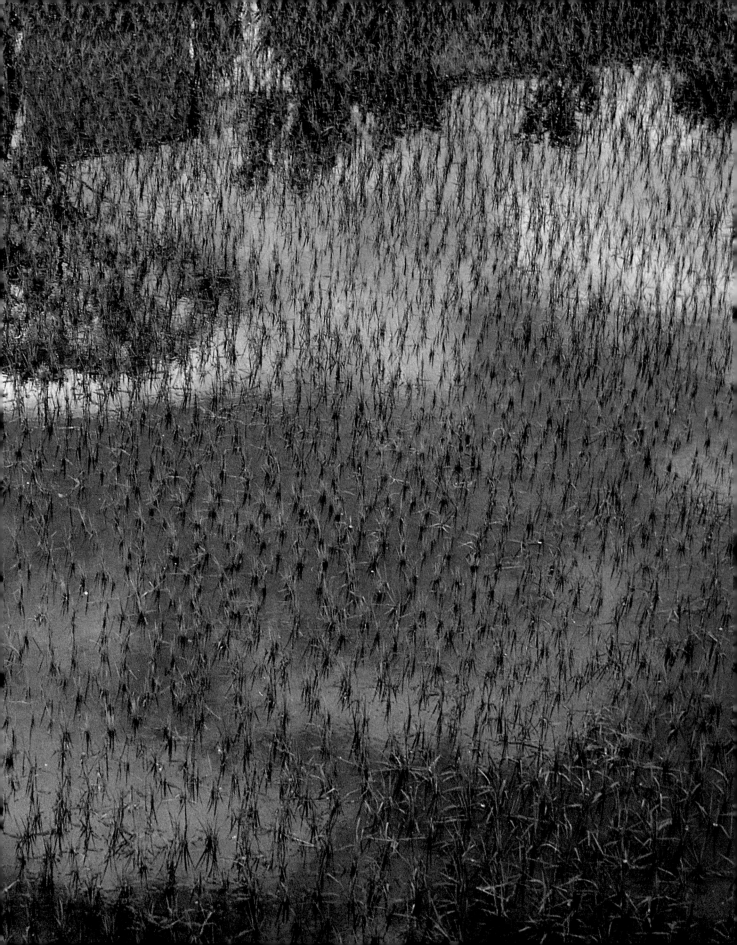

client: **Chrysler-Plymouth**
agency: Bozell Jacobs Kenyon & Eckhardt Inc.
art director: John Short
location: Georgia, California, Idaho, Michigan

We went out to do a little slice of Americana—the brief was to shoot twelve different situations. When we met the art director in California he said, "You know, I don't think you have to do those twelve situations. We'd like you to just go around the country and shoot anything you want, and we'll work from that." I said, "That's wonderful. But I want to do the twelve different situations, because I know that when we get back to New York they're going to ask where those twelve situations are." And that's just what we did. They never told me exactly what to shoot, except in so far as what they wanted it to be about. We did the welding shot in Detroit in the plant, and we did a boxing shot. They were also doing a TV assignment, and the TV guy would set up a whole shoot and I would shoot off him. We worked together. I was able to save the company a lot of money by doing things that he couldn't do while he was doing the things that he had to do. They rented a boxing gym and set it up and filled it with smoke and I was able to just walk in and shoot.

The car shot was a setup. For all these kinds of shoots you must have model releases from everybody, which I got as we went across the country.

client: **Royal Viking Cruise Line**
art director: Goodby Berlin Silverstein
agency: Rich Silverstein
location: Puerto Rico, Trinidad, Grenada

The assignment was to photograph the *Royal Viking* and make it look wonderful. When you have a helicopter you have a great deal of ease in following the ship: you know where it is, you go after it, you can speed, you can go slow. But the agency didn't want to do that kind of thing. So we had a logistical problem in keeping up with the ship. In some cases we were able to contact it by radio and stay on the same channel; in other cases something went wrong with the radio and it went sailing into the sunset. We got it sailing into the sunset, but that is all we could get.

The client used maybe a dozen or more pictures, including these five. We're talking about the five blind men and the elephant—there are many ways to perceive a thing. And I tried not to view this like a proscenium theater with everyone in the audience looking at it, but rather to see it in the round, and to see it as a piece of sculpture. How does it look this way? How does it look that way? How does it look higher? How does it look lower? There just are so many ways one can look at it.

We were in Puerto Rico, we were in Trinidad—it took about seven days. It was not a long assignment. But it was fraught with logistical problems, like not being allowed to go on a dock in Trinidad because the police didn't want us to. Finally we went. Getting into Trinidad with our equipment was impossible unless we paid about $20,000, which we weren't about to do, so I went into the country with only three cameras, and lenses, and shot a lot that way—proving that you don't need all that equipment.

We had to show the ship as a beautiful little jewel. This was shot between 4:30 and 5:00 in the morning. The sun had not come up yet, and what we have here is that quality of light that happens after dawn but before sunrise—a beautiful kind of light. If this had been a black ship we never could have done it, but a white ship worked. It was very tough to shoot because you would normally want to use a tripod, but you can't on a boat, yet you're shooting at a very slow shutter speed.

50

This is a beauty shot, a three-quarters view of the front of the ship, and it's starting to look kind of sexy and sleek. The precedent for this photograph is the picture that Cassandre did of the *Normandie* for some posters in the 1930s. The ship went sailing into the sunset and there was no way to stop it. At one point we cut across the bow to signal the captain that we wanted him to stop, but he wasn't too thrilled with that idea, and steamed off. You have to remember that the schedule and the photographs are important to the art director and to me, but the captain has a schedule to keep that means arriving in the next port at a certain time.

We wanted a very sleek, streamlined shot, like this one, but in the other picture it looks more like a giant, monster thing—a completely different vehicle. It shows how huge the ship is, not how sleek it is. When I was shooting it I was thinking, "You know, this makes it look more like a tub. I want to try this anyway, because it may give a sense of immense size of the mother ship in *Star Wars*." There's an incredible mass and bulk to it. So we just tried shooting it in a lot of different ways. It was also a problem because we could never get our chase boat to keep up with this giant ship, so I would get one kind of picture, then as it came toward me and moved across my vision, I would get different kinds of pictures.

client: **H. J. Heinz**
art director: Corporate Graphics
agency: Bennett Robinson
location: New Guinea, Morocco, England, Holland

This was an incredible assignment from Heinz: to go around the world and shoot the harvest. They wanted to show the tomato crop in Lisbon, they wanted to show it in California, and they wanted to show it in Morocco. Now in Morocco and Lisbon there are exotic conditions. The tomatoes look wonderful in those countries. In the United States they don't look so good, so we shot it as an aerial in terms of color. In Lisbon we shot the people. The art director told us, "I don't want these pictures to look alike at all. I don't want it to be one field after another. I want it to be a different experience for the reader." So in some pictures all we have is pointing up into the sky, a picture of trees. Then we have tractors in fields, a field of onions, and

one of a family, another that's a close-up of the hands of a woman with tomatoes, another a tight close-up of mushrooms and a woman picking them in the background. It was the kind of annual report where you were at the mercy of seasons. We had to do it in two trips. In one trip we did one group of vegetables, another trip we did another.

Heinz is a very sophisticated client who does not require a literal interpretation. In the picture of the tractor, they're picking onions, and there's absolutely nothing interesting about it. You can't see the act of picking and you can't see the onions because they grow underground. But the light is incredible. I was extremely

fortunate because it was beautiful light. Prior to this I had done a field of cabbages also on the same day, in totally different light, and each one was right for the particular thing I was doing. When I was photographing apples in the Shenandoah Valley, they were all being picked by blacks who really didn't want to have their pictures taken, so I had to approach it in an abstract way. But in Sussex, England, we had this lady who was just a wonderful kind of English lady. They bring out tea and china when they take their tea break. We were able to focus on her. The woman with the basket was the cover of the annual report. That was a full day of working in the field with all these women.

Jay Maisel

Jay Maisel has long held a legendary status in the fiercely competitive field of commercial photography. He is one of the most highly regarded professionals in the areas of editorial, advertising, and annual-report photography, and his pictures have been published in virtually all of the world's leading magazines.

Maisel has earned the high esteem in which both colleagues and art directors hold him, and the near-reverence with which he is regarded by a younger generation of photographers. A perfectionist, he brings boundless enthusiasm and energy to every assignment, as well as an uncanny ability to find original, creative solutions to the most challenging conceptual or visual problems. Maisel is known for his intelligence, warmth, and the extroverted humor that he willingly shares with all around him.

A trademark of Maisel's work is the emphasis on color and natural light. He does not structure his photographs in advance, relying instead on his intuitive and visceral response to what happens in the moment. "Inspiration to me is a funny word," he says. "I think you wait to see what's there and then relate to it. It's more letting the thing talk to you and make its own demands upon you." He feels he does not do his best work when limited by an art director's or editor's script. "I don't believe in preconceiving." Rather, he prefers to solve the creative problem on site, to "go out empty as you can be," free to respond to whatever miracle the moment offers. "If you go out with a solution in mind," he says, "you see only what you want to see."

In addition to the work he does on assignment, Maisel continually photographs for himself. Unlike many photographers, Maisel refuses to make a disparaging distinction between the work that he does as personal expression and that made for commercial purposes, for he brings the same creativity to the art of making photographs, regardless of how they will eventually be used. Maisel is passionately committed to seeing—and to helping us see—the world in a new way.

Born in Brooklyn, New York, in 1931, Maisel became interested in the visual arts—particularly graphic design—in high school, where he studied with Leon Friend, a teacher who changed his life. After graduating he studied privately with the painter Joseph Hirsch in 1949. He spent three years at New York's Cooper Union, then received a BFA in painting from Yale University, where he studied with noted Bauhaus painter Josef Albers. It was at Cooper Union that he became interested in photography. He intensely studied Andreas Feininger's books on photography, and in 1956 took a seminar taught by the legendary art director Alexey Brodovitch.

Maisel began his photographic career in 1954, working free-lance for magazines, advertising agencies, and international corporations. He has taught color photography at New York's School of Visual Arts and Cooper

Union; lectures extensively across the country; and conducts photography workshops at the Maine Photography Workshop and Anderson Ranch, as well as private workshops at his studio.

Numerous journals have featured articles about Maisel and his approach to photography, among them *The Christian Science Monitor*, *American Photographer*, *Du*, *Popular Photography*, *Camera 35*, *Photo*, and *Life*. His work has been exhibited widely in group and individual exhibitions. His show "Light on America," held at New York's International Center for Photography in 1986, was described by the Center's director, Cornell Capa, as one of the most highly attended exhibitions ever held there. Books include *Jerusalem* (1976), *San Francisco* (1972), *The Greatest Jewish City in the World* (1972), *I Grandi fotografi Jay Maisel* (1982), *America, America* (1983), *Light on America* (1986), and *The Most Beautiful Place in the World* (1986; editor and contributor).

Maisel has received many awards, including one for Outstanding Achievement in Photography from ASMP, the American Society of Magazine Photographers (1978). Eight years later the ASMP honored him as Photographer of the Year (1986). Maisel was also awarded the International Center of Photography's Infinity Award for Applied Photography (1987) and the Gold Medal for Photography by the Art Directors' Club of New York (1986 and 1987).

Technical information   Maisel began his career using both Hasselblad 2¼-inch and 35mm cameras, however today he uses 35mm cameras exclusively, and prefers the Nikon system. A typical assignment would find him with five Nikons, a motor-driven camera, and an array of lenses. He shoots approximately thirty to forty rolls of film a day. Maisel "brackets" his pictures, shooting the same scene in a variety of exposures to allow for variables in light, film speed, and processing. Although Maisel is expert in the use of artificial and strobe lighting, he prefers to use natural light whenever possible. His images are totally unmanipulated, and he is rare among color photographers in that he almost never uses filters to achieve his striking and unusual color effects. Although during the first ten years Maisel photographed in black and white, today he shoots almost exclusively in color. He has used either Kodachrome 25 or Kodachrome 64 color positive film for over 99 percent of his work.

Maisel lives and works out of a six-story, seventy-two-room converted bank building located on the Bowery in downtown New York. He maintains an archive of his work in an extensive filing system of well over a million slides that he keeps in a climate-controlled former bank vault in his studio.